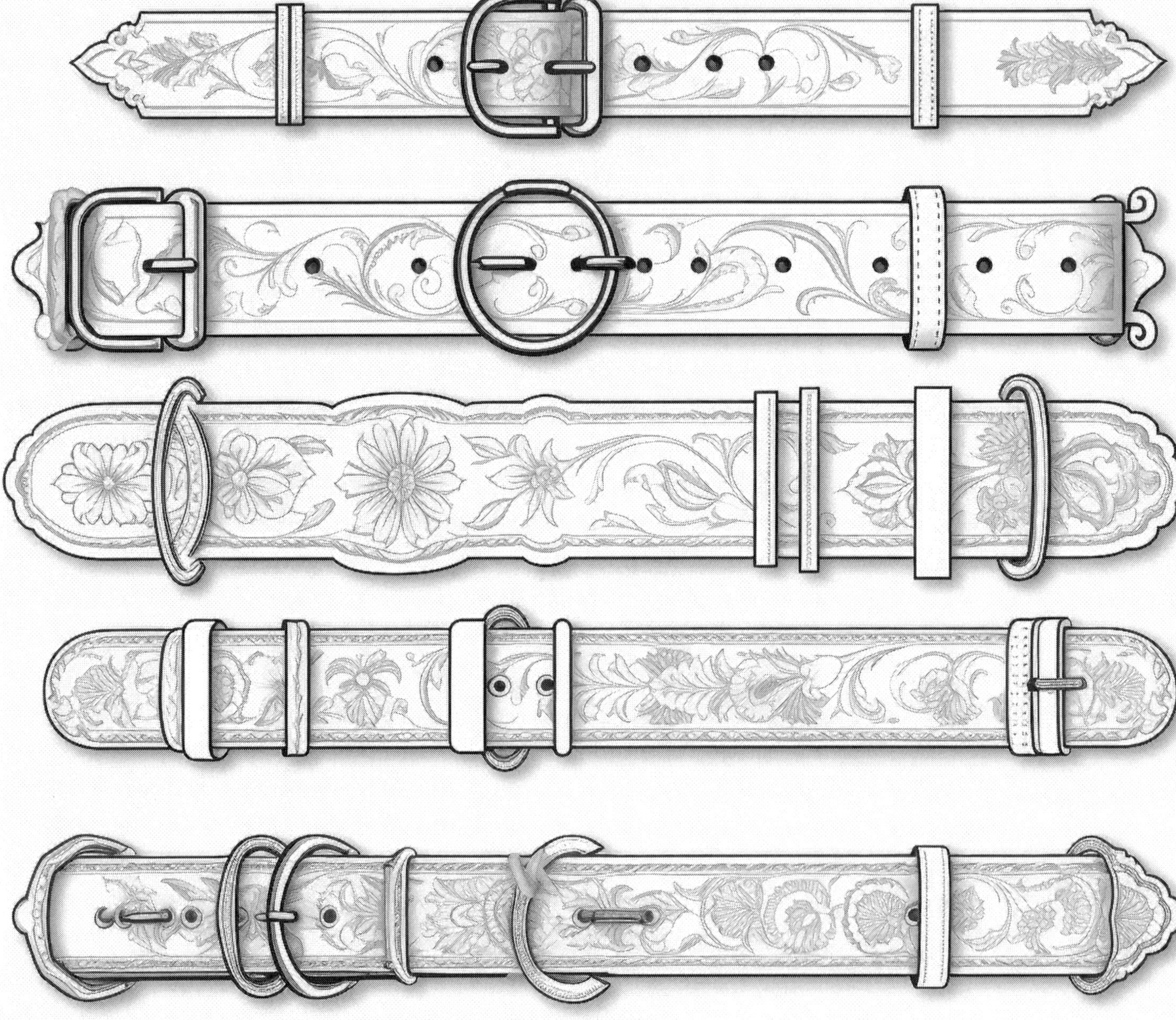

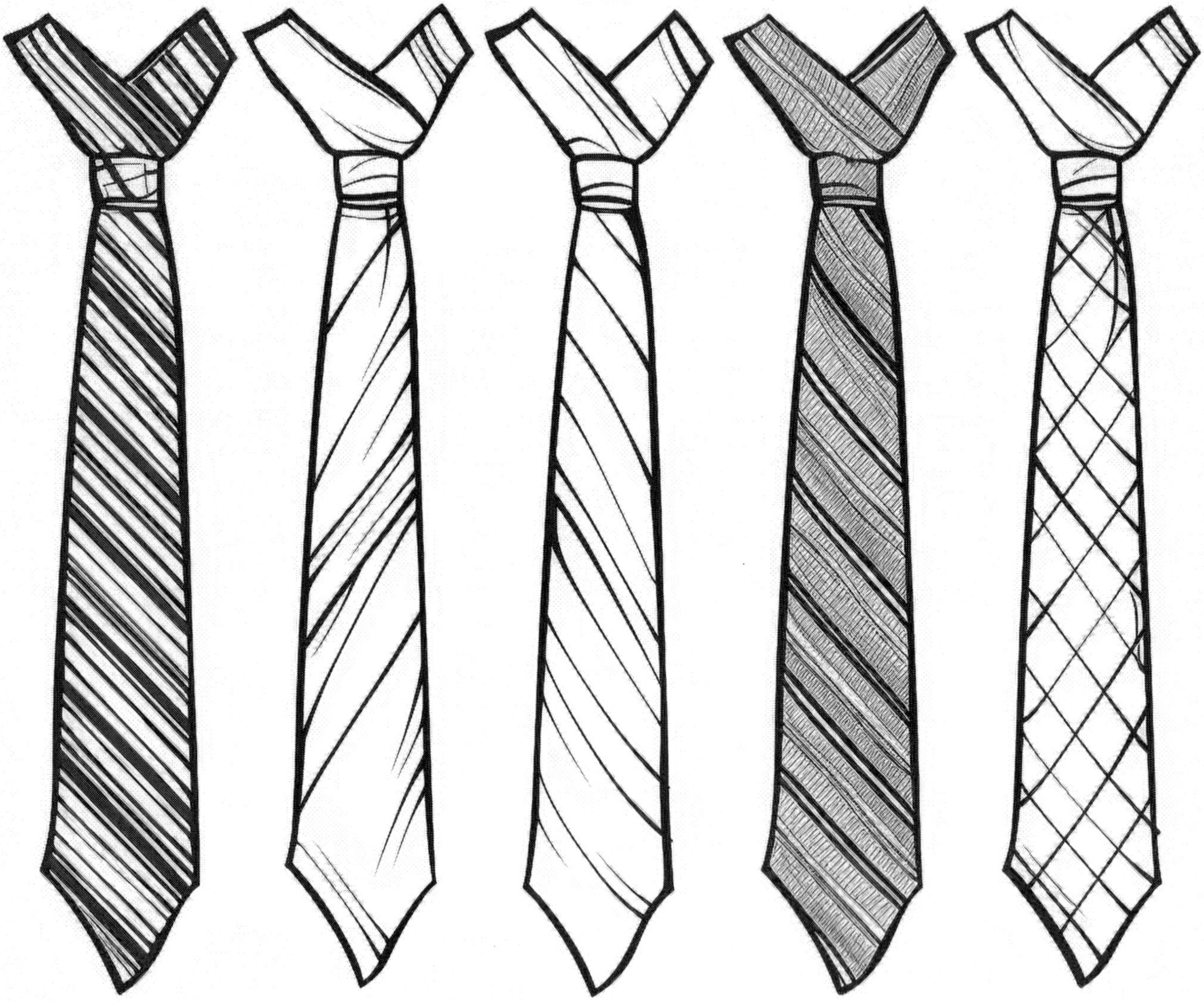

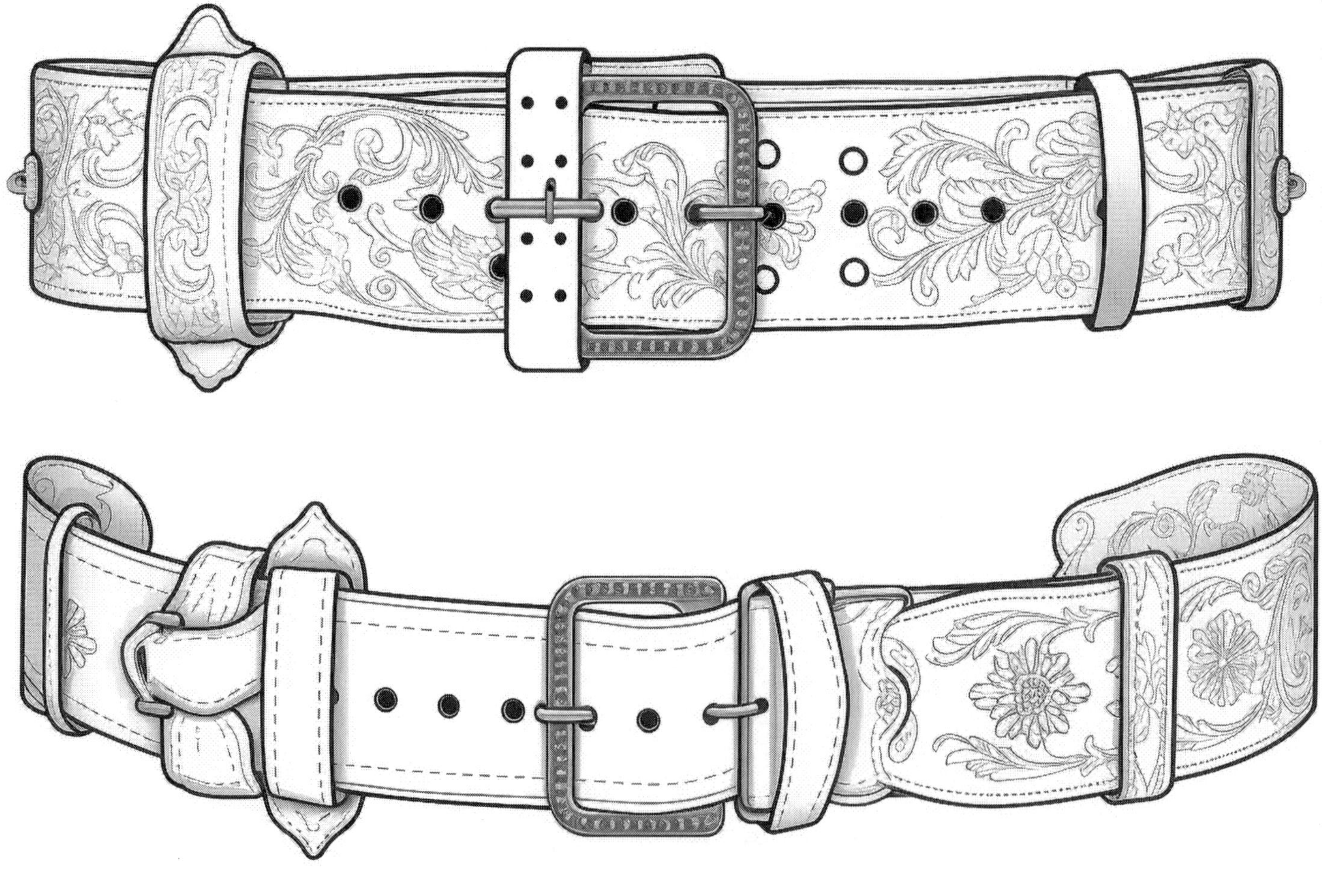

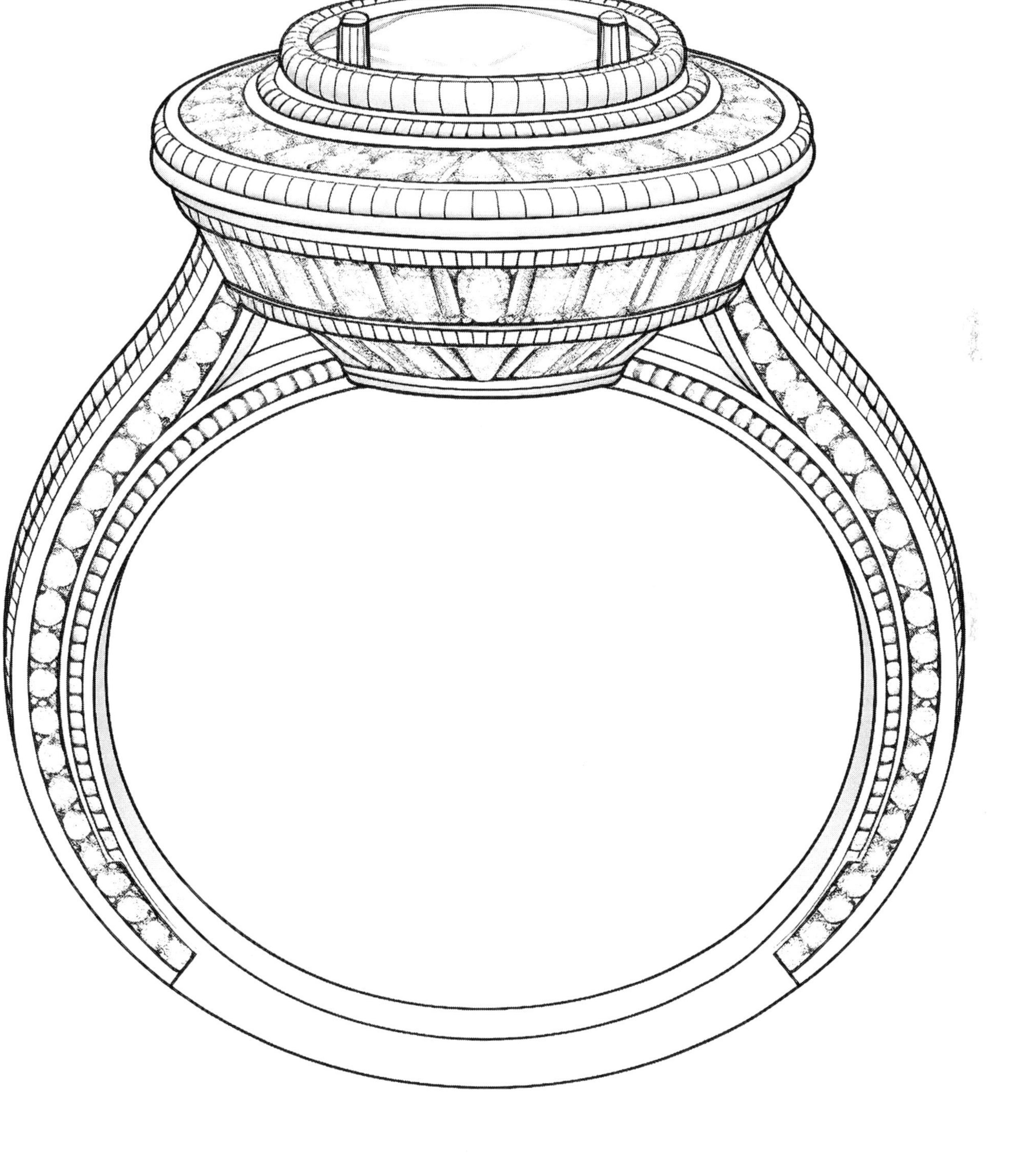

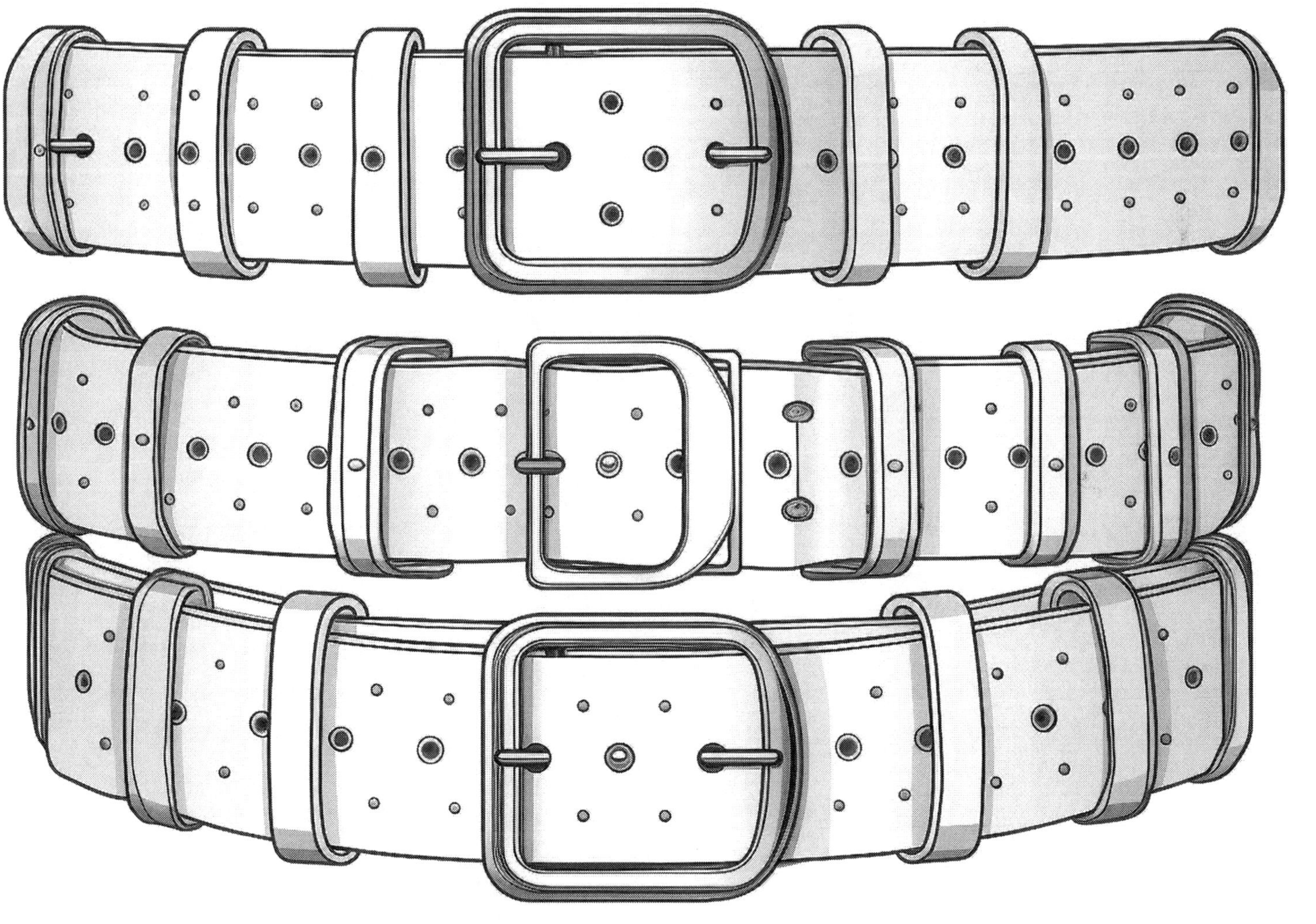

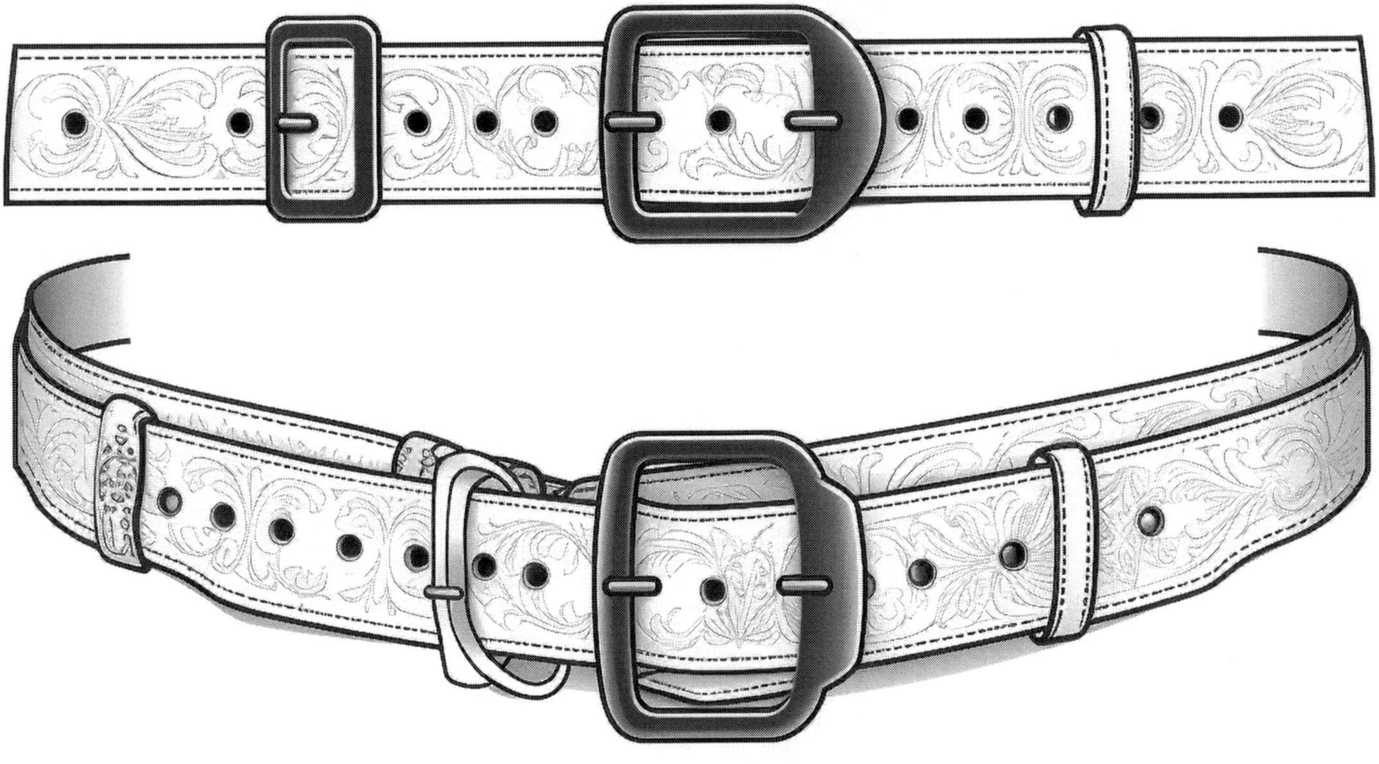

Made in the USA
Columbia, SC
14 July 2024

38594988R10057